PITMAN'S "SIMPLY EXPLAINED" SERIES

CAMOUFLAGE SIMPLY EXPLAINED

BY
Lt.-Col. CYRIL H. SMITH

The Naval & Military Press Ltd

Published by

The Naval & Military Press Ltd
Unit 5 Riverside, Brambleside
Bellbrook Industrial Estate
Uckfield, East Sussex
TN22 1QQ England

Tel: +44 (0)1825 749494

www.naval-military-press.com
www.nmarchive.com

*In reprinting in facsimile from the original, any imperfections are inevitably reproduced
and the quality may fall short of modern type and cartographic standards.*

PREFACE

THERE are many things a man must learn when he sets out to assist in the defence of his country.

How to handle the "tools" of war that he is given is, of course, the first consideration, and much can be done to make a man proficient in the use of weapons, but how long he will remain an effective user of these arms will depend largely, in the case of Home Guards, on the man's ability to see and not be seen.

Appreciation of the art of concealment is a factor which applies to fighters in the air as well as those who will come to grips with the enemy on the ground. Hence this booklet is intended as a guide both to the Home Guard and to the A.T.C.

The big-game hunter has learnt by experience not only to make sure that the shot he fires will kill, but to be able to approach his objective unseen, and to be able to read signs and tracks.

It is not necessary to be a big-game hunter or to have been born in the country to understand the art, though undoubtedly the modern town-dweller has not only lost the habit but has to a great extent become ignorant of the method of hiding by instinct.

War revives the need for concealment.

The Home Guard must conceal himself and his post if he is to have any chance of surprising the enemy. The wide range, speed and accuracy of the aeroplane and its camera have made concealment much more difficult, and in some cases elaborate measures involving considerable expenditure of time and material will be required before the desired result is obtained. None the less, most cases will call for only common sense and judgment.

PREFACE

To the embryo airman in the A.T.C. an understanding of the methods used as aids to individual concealment, and the hiding of signs of military activity, will be of great value when the time comes for him to take his place in the ranks of the Royal Air Force. If he knows the methods he will be less likely to be deceived.

When any work of concealment is to be done forethought will always indicate the course to adopt, but owing to the speed of modern battle there may not be time to do much, and concealment must therefore become an ingrained and automatic habit.

This can be done by an understanding of the principles and constant practice and discipline in their application.

CYRIL H. SMITH

CAMOUFLAGE
SIMPLY EXPLAINED

THE word camouflage comes no doubt from the French *camouflet*, and the original meaning was, therefore, "Puffing smoke into someone's face." In this sense we may use the word to mean blinding enemy observation. Camouflage proper may be defined as concealment of the act, or the fact that something is being concealed. It is the science of deceit and deception, and does not mean hiding in the accepted sense. At the present time instruction in the art holds a high position in the training curricula of the armed forces, and it is also a very necessary part of the training of Home Guard personnel. Concealment is a primitive instinct among wild creatures and uncivilized peoples—it is an automatic habit—because upon the individual ability to do so effectively depends their very existence.

Civilized people and particularly town-dwellers have lost the need, and with it the art, of concealment, and it is therefore necessary for members of the Home Guard to re-learn what to their ancestors would have been a natural habit, a habit upon which their lives depended when in daily conflict with the wild beasts of the field.

Perfect camouflage of any work can be attained only by non-interference with the normal or natural aspect of the locality because this is the aspect with which the enemy has no doubt become familiar by the use of photographs taken during peace time. It must be remembered that it is essential for work to be concealed from observation *both from the air and from the ground*.

In the last great war camouflage was not so important as it is to-day, because observation was mostly visual and cameras were not so efficient and were unable to photograph such detail as they do now. An aerial photograph of to-day in the hands of an expert will tell a complete story, showing defence positions, barbed wire, gun emplacements, and all the marks on the land of the activities of war.

Photographs can be taken either directly above an

FIG. 1. Frogs and toads are examples of how Nature protects creatures with a skin pattern that will conceal them from their enemies. Note how the vulnerable point, the eye, is hidden in a patch of dark in a light design

object or showing a partial side view. The former are called "verticals." The latter are known as "obliques," and it is these which enable the expert to estimate heights of walls and buildings, or even depths of anti-tank ditches.

To prevent the experts who study these photographs from gaining knowledge of the defences of this country the use of camouflage is essential. Therefore every Home Guard should study the technique used for special purposes as occasion demands.

Camouflage is not a highly skilled science, and it is a mistake to think that artists alone are capable of good camouflage work. Only in the most exceptional cases should the services of a specially trained operator be necessary. Camouflage is the exercise of common sense, imagination and attention to detail, and, what is most important, an appreciation of how Nature assists its creatures in self-preservation.

Knowledge of animal life and experience of woodcraft are of great help when preparing camouflage, as nearly

FIG. 2. The zebra in its natural surroundings is concealed

every creature has been given some protective colour which will blend with its surroundings (see Fig. 1). Moreover, a great many animals and birds appear to have a very good knowledge of colour and backgrounds as when danger is present they seem to be able to make themselves inconspicuous, and by remaining motionless they escape detection.

The most perfect example of this natural assistance is seen in the zebra. The stripes on his body help him to merge into the background of the land that he inhabits (Fig. 2). But if he is put against a very different background the contrast is alarming (Fig. 3). Again, if the white polar bear were taken from his natural surroundings he would be most conspicuous.

The tiger and the giraffe are other examples of animals

Fig. 3. Taken from its natural home, it becomes conspicuous

that have a disruptive pattern on their skins or hair which aids them in concealment. Obviously, the study of animals and their skin patterns will assist in planning camouflage work.

There is one further aspect from which a lesson can be learned. Certain animals and most fish have the underside of their bodies a much lighter shade than their backs (see Fig. 4). In the case of beasts of the fields the deeper the shadow the more they tend to show up when viewed from above. Nature has accordingly provided them with a means of destroying their shape by reducing the depth of shadow by giving them white bellies.

Fish are white underneath so that when viewed from below by their enemies the whiteness merges into the lightness of the shallow water and the sun shining down.

FIG. 4. The blue shark, showing white underside and dark top to assist in concealment

On the other hand their backs are very dark green—almost blue-black in some cases—and when viewed from above in shallow water fish so coloured will be practically invisible. An appreciation of this natural colouring seen against certain backgrounds will very materially assist the student of camouflage.

The details that give information to the enemy airman or ground observer can be grouped under six main headings. The principles enunciated can be applied to the concealment of positions, buildings, vehicle parks and all types of defence works. The headings are as follows—

1. Colour or texture.
2. Shadow and shine.
3. Characteristic shape.
4. Repetition.
5. Tracks.
6. Movement.

COLOUR

Each colour has its tonal quality, and all colours can be raised or lowered in tone. In a landscape, however, what tends to alter the colours is not so much the tonal differences as the influence of shadows. Depth of tone is essentially controlled by the amount of shadow on an area.

To the high flying observer and the aerial camera the ground is seen in terms of tone, but in a photograph all is monochrome and at a height colours tend to lose their identity. More than by colour, then, the tone of the background is decided by the texture, and by texture is meant the permanent shadow content of the ground surface.

Tall standing grass will show up much darker than very short grass although of exactly the same colour, owing to the deep shadows in the thousands of blades of long grass. This effect can be readily seen when brushing the skin of a silk hat or the cloth upon a billiard table.

A field of young corn when seen from a distance at ground level may appear light green, but if viewed from the air on a windless day probably only the earth would be seen, darker than usual owing to the shadows of the young corn.

An appreciation of the colour or texture of the background is therefore essential in the business of concealment. In addition, the pattern of the landscape must be learnt. It is, of course, impossible for everyone who will have to carry out camouflage to fly over the area where he will have to fight, but nevertheless a mental effort must be made to acquire a bird's eye view of the local pattern, as it is into this pattern that the concealed position or building will have to fit.

SHADOW AND SHINE

Every object standing alone in sunlight throws a shadow which may attract the enemy's attention more quickly than the object itself.

Shadows will show on a photograph what the object is, even though the actual object itself cannot be seen, and "obliques" will present the enemy with a portrait of the object in black and white. (See Fig. 5.)

When thinking out ideas for concealment of shadows it must be borne in mind that owing to the apparent movement of the sun around the object the shadow will also move. The area of travel of the shadow should be

FIG. 5. Shadows show up what is there without the object being seen. This illustrates clearly the danger of shadows

noted, and if the ground is flat and level this evenness must be destroyed. By producing a very broken surface the shape of the shadow can be considerably altered.

Heaps of cinders or similar material placed around the position or object will prevent a true shadow being cast.

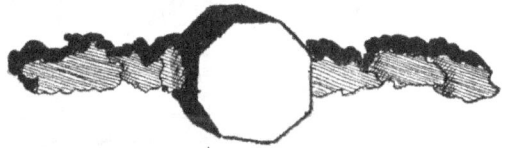

FIG. 6. Showing how shadows of pill-boxes without any treatment for concealment or camouflage would show up to air observation

Paint can also be used to put false shadows on all sides, and designs can be used which will hide completely the true shadow (see Figs. 6 and 7).

A net which has strips of canvas threaded into it, that

is to say, one garnished with hessian strip, can be used to hide the shadow by carrying it over the object and having it pegged to the ground away from the object.

FIG. 7. How the pill-box may be treated to merge into the background, by disruptive painting upon the roof and ground to "lose" the shadows

Nets can be used for hiding the shadows cast by guns or vehicles or the effects of gun blast outside weapon pits by stretching them on poles above the object to be concealed (see Fig. 8).

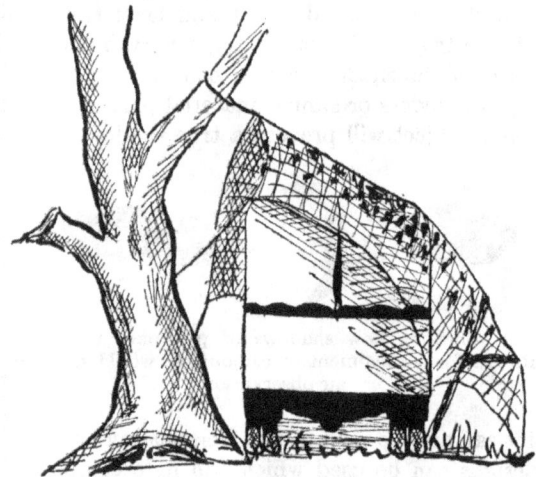

FIG. 8. Nets that are used to cover vehicles should be stretched out and held away from them so that the outline is concealed

The garnishing of nets must be done carefully (see page 30) and the colour of the canvas strips used must tone with the colour of the background in the vicinity of the defence position. Nets are supplied to the Home Guard, but plain chicken netting used with strips of sacking would serve the same purpose.

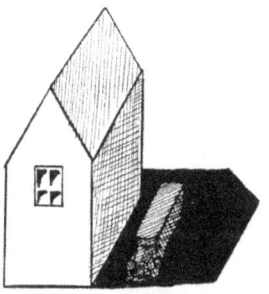

FIG. 9. When using shadows as cover do not forget that they move round with the sun. If parking a vehicle, be prepared to move it often if it must remain hidden

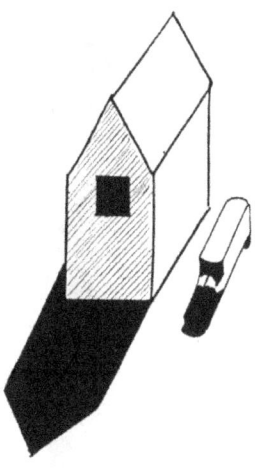

Vehicles when parked at the side of a road should be so placed that their shadows do not show their position. Have them put so that their shadows will die away into the grass verge or roadside, and if it is possible park them on the verge itself so that any shadow will be hidden by hedge or buildings (see Fig. 10). Failure to take this elementary precaution is a mistake often made by experienced drivers of the regular army.

Shine is another great source of danger. Shine is the quality of reflecting light possessed by all smooth surfaces. Even in dry weather shine may reveal with the utmost clearness buildings, vehicles, and men that in all other ways are admirably concealed. Steel helmets, tops of vehicles, roofs of buildings, windscreens, men's glasses, and all flat asphalt or concrete surfaces where light can strike directly will reveal a complete picture to an observer.

FIG. 10. Park vehicles in such positions that their shadows will not disclose them. If possible park them on the grass verge and on the shadow side of the road so that they merge into the surroundings

In wet weather the danger is greatly increased, and every effort must be made to prevent or reduce shine by using a flat paint in which is mixed sand or cork dust. Alternatively, tar can be used with sand thrown onto the surface while the tar is still wet.

This tar treatment should be given to concrete roads, but only portions of the road should be done as the result

CAMOUFLAGE SIMPLY EXPLAINED 11

desired is the breaking up of the white straight line ordinarily indicating a road.

Home Guards should remember particularly their waterproof and anti-gas capes and steel helmets. For

FIG. 11. A defence post without any attempt at camouflage as seen from the air and from the ground

FIG. 12. The same post after disruptive paint has hidden the shape and given a good chance of freedom from observation

these they have been issued with small string nets coloured dark green and brown. If a net is put on a steel helmet that has been painted with a gritty matt paint there will be no chance of any reflection of light from that particular helmet either in wet or dry weather.

CHARACTERISTIC SHAPE

This is the generally accepted shape of such things as water towers, gas-holders, etc., that go to make up the everyday view of the man in the street. If he catches a glimpse of only a small portion of a certain object, the shape of that portion tells him what the total object is. The modern concrete factory with its flat roof and many

 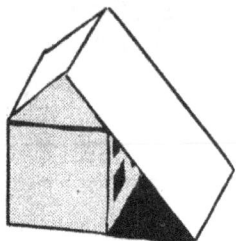

FIG. 13. Canvas screens can be used to destroy the shapes of buildings by continuing the slope of the roof to the ground. They also hide the shadows and give good vehicle cover

windows would immediately tell the observer what was there even though the greater part was obscured by trees.

If complete concealment is to be achieved the characteristic shape must be destroyed and there are many ways of accomplishing this.

The method most commonly used for large buildings, pill-boxes, chimneys, and similar structures is by what is called "disruptive" painting. This is the painting of a bold large pattern across the object to be concealed, always bearing in mind that the aim must be to break up the outline against a variety of backgrounds. (See Figs. 11 and 12.)

Again must be stressed the absolute necessity of fitting the design into the tone and shape of the surroundings.

Canvas stretched between the gables of a building and also from the eaves of a roof following the same slope

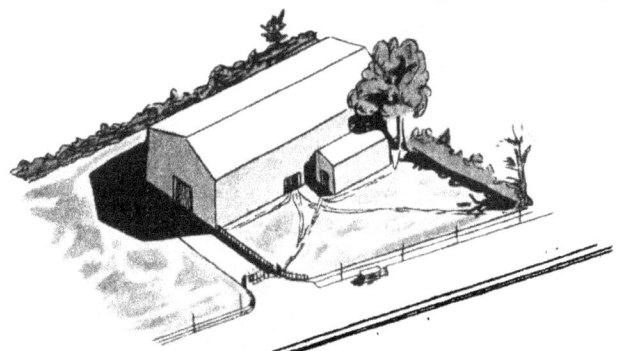

FIG. 14. How a factory would look from the air

FIG. 15. How it would appear after skilful treatment with paint and the use of canvas screens

pegged to the ground away from the building will destroy and, as previously mentioned, help to hide any shadow. (See Figs. 13, 14, and 15.)

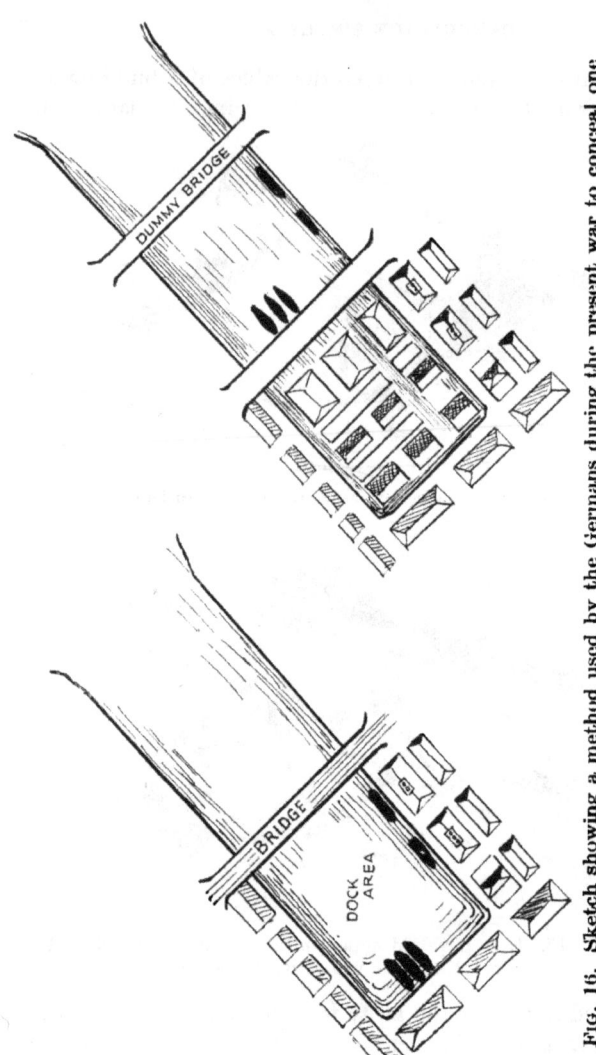

FIG. 16. Sketch showing a method used by the Germans during the present war to conceal one of their docks from bombing by the R.A.F. Barges were put in the dock area and over them was stretched canvas upon which was painted a pattern to fit in with the surrounding warehouses

CAMOUFLAGE SIMPLY EXPLAINED 15

Fig. 16 is a good example of the method used by the Germans to conceal a dock area.

Pill-boxes lend themselves to camouflage as they can be painted to suit the background. Trees and bushes in

FIG. 17. A pill-box defence position as it would appear without any attempt at concealment of camouflage

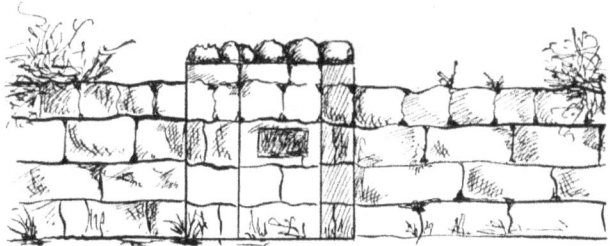

FIG. 18. The same after being "lost" in the background by the aid of paint. The wall design is continued across the post, and stones or pieces of concrete are put on the roof to destroy the shape

the background can be continued across the pill-box and when viewed from ground level will appear to be a part of the wood itself. (See also Figs. 17 and 18.)

The colours used should be warm. Dark greens, browns and yellows are all suitable, but the exact shades will depend upon local conditions. Outlining the colours with black is a waste of effort and of no value. The darker colours must predominate above and the lighter colours below. Oilbound paints should not be used.

The edge of the building or object must not stand in relief against the background but must receive attention

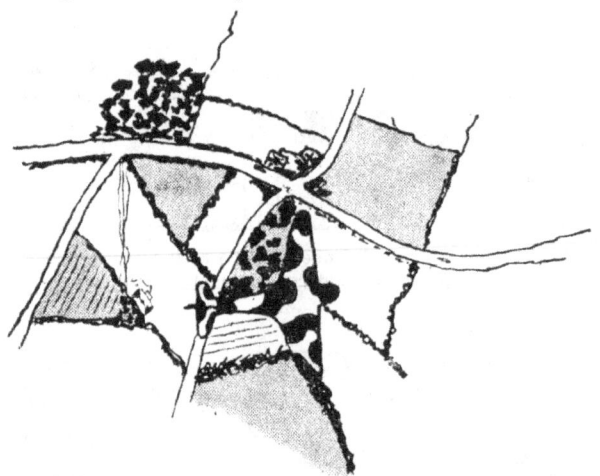

FIG. 19. How an aeroplane treated with disruptive paint might appear when observed from another aircraft flying above it

so that the shape is destroyed, and any shadows on the object itself must be toned to the surroundings.

When planning any camouflage work that entails fitting into a background it must be remembered that there are seasons of the year, that trees bud and come into leaf in the spring, and then in the autumn and winter the leaves fall. Consequently, if a design is painted which incorporates leaves and blooms it must be altered at the correct time.

Aeroplanes also have a characteristic shape, and in camouflaging them this must be destroyed. In this case there is a difference because an aeroplane must be concealed from observation from below as well as be made as inconspicuous as possible from an enemy flying above.

Aeroplanes have their upper surfaces treated with a disruptive pattern of such a nature that whether on the ground or flying over the countryside they fit into the pattern of the background (see Fig. 19). Here it is well

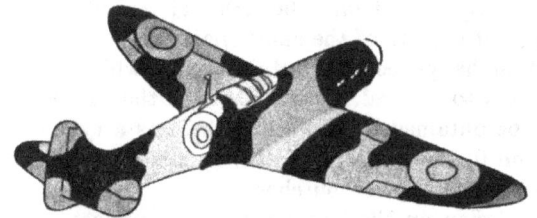

FIG. 20. The disruptive pattern normally used on aircraft that fly over Britain

to remember that a machine painted to suit the English pattern with its many earth patches showing up as a motley design would not be at all suitable if stood upon an aerodrome in the East that is mostly sand. (See Fig. 20.)

The underside also is painted in shades of blue and silver—a light eggshell blue for summer and a much darker blue-grey for winter. Here again much depends upon the climatic conditions of the country over which the plane will have to fly.

REPETITION

With this feature we can also class regularity as anything in a landscape that is regular is invariably a sign of man's handiwork.

Battery positions are often given away by the regular spacing of the guns. Similarly the regular spacing of tents in camps betrays them. In both cases, however careful their concealment it is not as a rule possible to avoid some indication on an aerial photograph which will show up as a series of marks that invite attention.

Nature does not repeat itself, and therefore in using camouflage to conceal positions the design or shape must not be repeated.

It is easy to fall into the habit of repetition when a number of objects of the same shape have to be camouflaged, as happened in a certain county which had many pill-boxes to conceal. It was thought that a good effect could be obtained by disguising these as a type of kiosk common in this country at railway stations where books and cigarettes can be purchased.

The design on the first pill-box was perfect and completely carried out its purpose of concealing the fact that it was a strong post; it looked just like a shut-up kiosk. The whole of the scheme was spoilt by repeating this same design all over the county. But the greatest error of all was to put it round pill-boxes that were in the middle of fields and other places where, of course, no kiosks would ever be!

Even now army vehicles can be seen in convoy with their canvas hoods and covers all painted in one and the same design. Repetition or regularity should at all costs be avoided if good concealment is to be achieved.

TRACKS

Air reconnaissance sets out to test the enemy defences, his strength and depth. The resulting reports and photographs are very carefully studied, and it may help if we consider upon what evidence the experts who study these reports and photographs base their deductions as to the strength or disposition of enemy troops or guns,

CAMOUFLAGE SIMPLY EXPLAINED

A heap of spoil, that is, freshly turned earth, or a patch of bare earth, which shows up white upon a photograph, in itself indicates little though it may mark a gun post, a single hut or a host of other things, but the expert will invariably find contributory evidence which enables him to tell exactly what the patch represents.

Buried telephone cable betrays itself because disturbed earth takes a long time to settle down again and will show up on a photograph.

Again, where Danert wire has been put round a position, cattle will graze up to the wire but the grass inside the wire will remain long and, as already mentioned, will appear darker on the photograph. Hence a ring will be seen surrounding something.

The amount of traffic that has used a certain track across a field can be seen in an aerial photograph, and if the tracks finish at a house or farm it will no doubt receive attention as being of importance. Track discipline is something that Home Guards must learn as they have a semi-static role which necessitates their taking up positions in pill-boxes, slit trenches, weapon pits and certain other sites at which will be placed the particular weapons issued to them. In going to and from these positions unless great care is taken they will be disclosed even though the posts themselves are concealed (see Fig. 21).

Tracks to positions should follow along hedges, ditches and fences, and where possible be on the shadow side (see Fig. 22). A well-concealed path can be made where plough land joins grass. The shortest way is very often the most dangerous, and some thought must be given to the best way of approach.

If a position being used is in the centre of a field, the track should leave the road and pass along a hedge or join of plough and grass, then direct to the position,

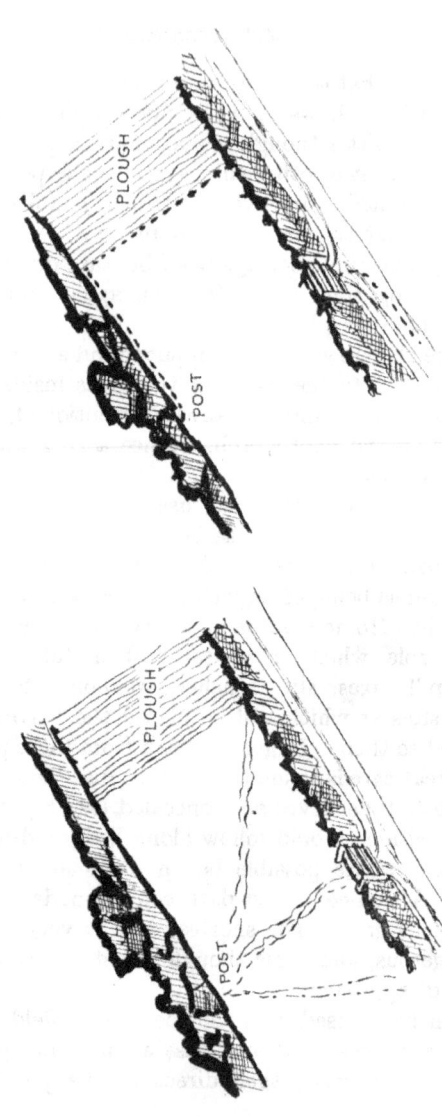

FIG. 21. Tracks denote to the enemy the position of defence posts. Short cuts clearly reveal the position

FIG. 22. Example of track discipline. The track is concealed by following the hedge and field boundary

passing as near to the entrance as possible. From that point a false track, which must always be kept fresh, should be continued to the edge of the field. Then, if the position has been well camouflaged, it will not appear

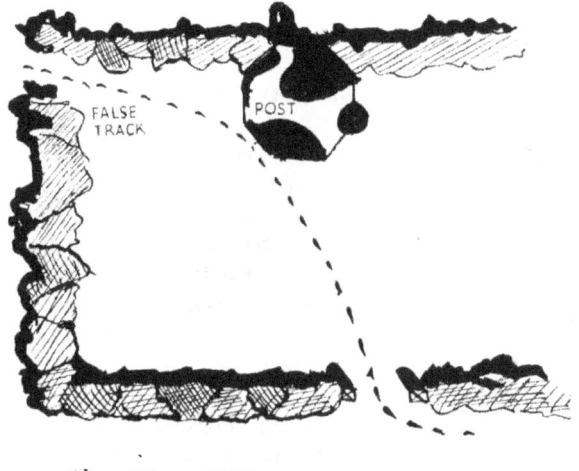

FIG. 23. A false track should always be made so that a position is not given away by the sudden cessation of a track

that the tracks lead anywhere than across the field (Fig. 23).

Spoil from any digging at the position can be used along the false path.

Widening of the path to the post should not be allowed. Decoy tracks can be used leading off in another direction to a badly camouflaged dummy post to draw enemy fire and enable the proper post to make a surprise attack.

If vehicles have to visit your post or Headquarters do not let their tyre tracks denote your position. A branch of a tree tied behind a lorry when it leaves the post will remove most traces of the fact that a vehicle has been there. During the present war the attention of our troops in France to this detail of track discipline around some Brigade Headquarters saved them from the aerial attack to which otherwise they would have been subjected.

MOVEMENT

An observer's eye will always be attracted to a point of movement.

In dealing with this aspect of concealment, the conduct of the birds and beasts of the field is worthy of notice. When they think that they are being observed they stay quite still, or, as it is called, "freeze." American Indians had this ability developed to a marked degree, and they were able to stay fixed in any position for a long enough time to allow an observer's eye to pass over the spot where he may have thought he saw movement.

Movement itself cannot be camouflaged or concealed. Its effect can only be minimized. For example, a car park can have netting suspended above it in order to help to conceal the moving lorries underneath.

Lorries moving along roads, even though painted with a good disruptive pattern, will not in any way be concealed unless they stop and take up a position against a reasonable background.

Fig. 24 shows how during the last war the Germans managed to hide for a considerable time the place where they were repairing their aircraft and other plant.

Over a large stretch of country was stretched canvas well above the ground like a huge flat-topped factory, and upon the canvas was painted the pattern of the original country roads and hedges. Photographs failed for some time to reveal the fact that there was anything untoward there; even obliques did not show any "join" of roof

CAMOUFLAGE SIMPLY EXPLAINED. 23

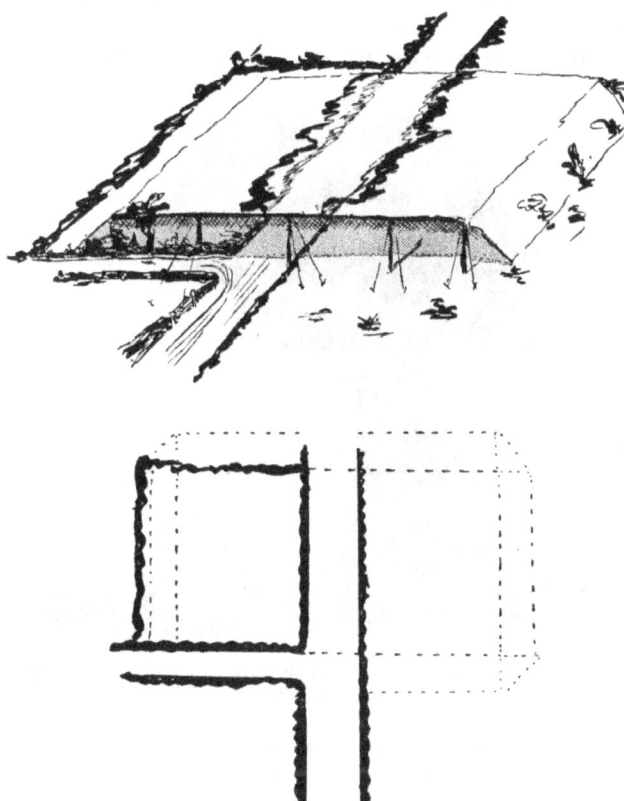

FIG. 24. Method used by the Germans in the last war to conceal a repair depot. The two sketches indicate how it would have appeared in an oblique and a vertical photograph respectively

and ground as the roof sloped down and the pattern continued.

Many reports were received that lorries seemed to

Fig. 25. Although the man is in deep shadow he is easily seen against the background

disappear suddenly at a certain point, and this was explained only when the place was eventually captured.

PERSONAL CAMOUFLAGE

The present-day soldier must be invisible to the enemy and must be able to fight from defensive posts that he has chosen himself. Upon his ability to learn the lessons of concealment will depend whether he and his section are blasted or not. Therefore he must be able to use cover, background and shadow, and he must be able to improvise simple aids to concealment.

The Home Guard wishing to specialize as a sniper or scout must train to "melt" into the background. In all the art of camouflage it is background that counts, and

Fig. 26. A patrol although well hidden below the skyline can be seen by their reflection in the water

appreciation of this truth will make a good soldier better. At night, keeping below the skyline does not necessarily ensure invisibility to the enemy. (See Figs. 25–27.)

The Home Guard can make a camouflaged suit very easily with an old sack or two pieces of canvas, and, when painted with a disruptive pattern suitable to the environment in which he expects to work, this will enable him to remain unseen. (See Fig. 28.)

The net issued to him for use with the steel helmet

should have foliage pushed into it (Fig. 29). If this is done correctly, the shape of the helmet will be hidden,

FIG. 27. A man's outline can be seen if it breaks into another texture even though it does not break the skyline

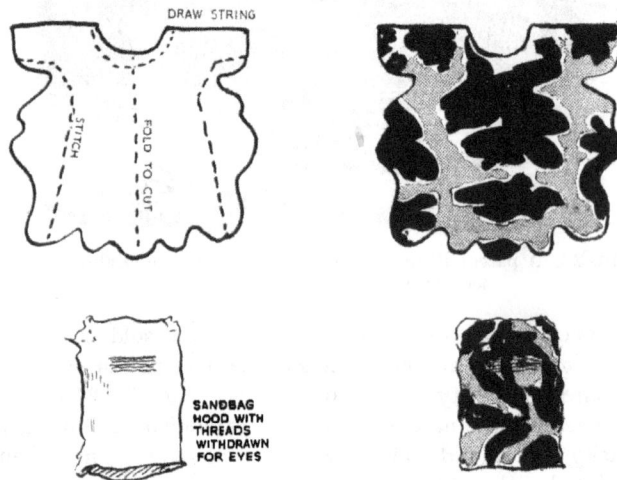

FIG. 28. Personal concealment

and provided the vegetation used is from the same locality observation can be safely carried out.

There are many other items of the soldier's uniform and person to be considered when preparations are being made for personal camouflage.

The face and hands can be seen from great distances

FIG. 29. The steel helmet with a rubber band held by two pieces of metal into which local vegetation can be put to cover and destroy the dome shape. The garnish should be hung well over the rim, and come over the neck and shoulders. If just one waving piece were used it would reveal the position

if not treated with burnt cork or mud. Alternatively, gloves can be worn on the hands. Whilst covering the face and hands do not forget the back of the neck, a point often missed when the enemy is only expected from the front. Concealment nowadays must take into account observation from any direction.

Boots should be covered with sacking and the rifle

should be similarly treated. If a strip of old sack is used it can be kept in place with rubber bands.

Pieces of old curtains dyed green or brown are of great assistance in covering the face and respirator, and these again help to break up the shape.

When making an observation never look up to the sky except through a net of some sort as the face can be seen from a great height. This is very important if your point of concealment is in an isolated position.

Vegetation to make a post should never be moved into a position where it normally would not be found. For example, a bush should not be uprooted and taken to the centre of a ploughed field.

If the helmet has been garnished in a valley with rushes from a river bank, do not forget to remove them when moving to a different locality. The mistake of leaving old and dead vegetation in the hat is often made and will give your position away to a keen observer.

MATERIALS TO USE FOR CAMOUFLAGE

As already indicated, the War Office have issued a certain amount of material for the purpose of carrying out the work of concealment, but the keen Home Guard, especially if in charge of a defence post, will wish to use what he can find locally. In doing so he may well produce a better job than with the issued materials.

Exactly what to use will, of course, be decided by the background and also the angle and distance from which enemy observation may be expected. These factors will fix whether purely natural means can be used, such as taking branches and local foliage, but consideration must be given to the length of time that the position should be capable of giving concealment without excessive maintenance.

The materials fall into three main groups—

(a) Disruptive painting, overhead nets, screens, dummy works and artificial mounds.

(b) Branches, turf, ashes and debris of all sorts and any scrap building materials that may be available.

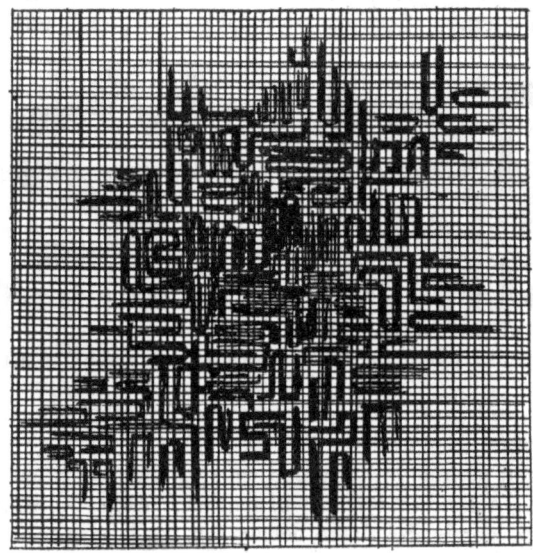

FIG. 30. How a net should be treated with canvas "scrim." The thickly garnished area must be large enough to cover the object to be concealed

(c) Sacking, hessian-canvas, matt paint, wire netting, fish nets and steel wool.

Since nets form the chief item of concealment in the army of to-day, it is worth while considering them in greater detail. They are of square mesh, and the size of the mesh varies with the work to which they are to be put. Some are large fish nets and others smaller.

The nets themselves are not capable of giving concealment, but act merely as a foundation to which is fixed the material which does give concealment. This material is called "scrim garnish," and consists of lengths of canvas of a suitable width. It is supplied in rolls in four colours—dark green, light green, earth and brown.

The method of garnishing must aim at giving sufficient

 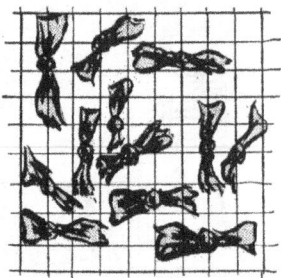

Fig. 31. Two methods of fixing strips of "scrim" to nets

cover and producing a surface that matches the background in tone and colour.

When used as an overhead cover it must be capable of casting a shadow which will neither outline the edge of the net nor by its shape betray the net's presence to an air observer.

Strips must be woven into the net flat as shown in Fig. 30 and should always go across the width of the mesh square and not across the corners. When thinning, strips should always point towards the edge of the net, but should never be taken close to the edge.

The thickly garnished part must be large enough to cover the object and extend far enough for the garnishing to be thinned out. The thinning should produce a starfish pattern. Fig. 31 shows two kinds of garnishing.

Steel wool is used for many purposes in camouflage work. It is normally coloured grass green or earth, but it can of course be sprayed any colour required. The wool will serve as a means of concealment much longer than any other material as it is not affected by the weather. It can be tufted to produce a high texture or

Fig. 32. A piece of wire netting to which are fixed strips of canvas will make a very effective screen to cover a rifleman. It can be fired through and it is also portable and can be garnished with local vegetation

can be kept smooth to match untextured surfaces. It is fireproof and transparent when viewed against the light.

Rifles can be fired through it, and it can be used to represent grass, plough, or trodden earth. It is the only known material which can be relied upon to defy point blank observation. It can be fixed to all types of nets, but gives the best results when used with wire netting.

Zinc mesh is also very useful as it can be formed into shapes representing sandbags or bricks. If painted to match the surroundings it will defy detection and will conceal observation peep holes in walls or in anything else through which it is desired to look without being seen.

THE LESSON

Any military activity leaves its story written upon the ground as a series of scars and tracks, and we must reduce to a minimum the amount of information yielded.

A margin of safety lies in the fact that to be of use to the enemy many photographs at frequent intervals would

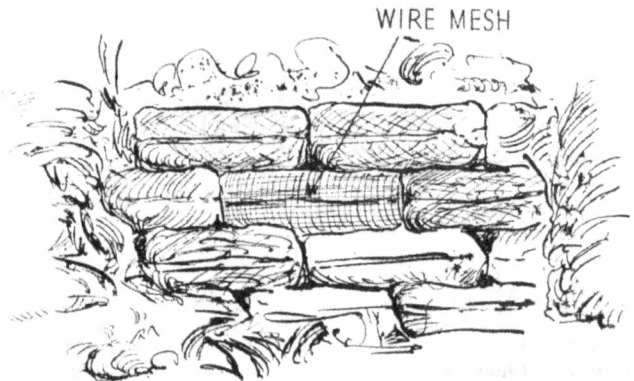

FIG. 33. Wire mesh painted to suit the surrounding area can be used in many ways to conceal look-outs

have to be taken, and they would need constant review to show any change that had taken place. Because of the speed of modern warfare this is, of course, impossible.

The main fundamental in concealment is not to catch the eye, as any sudden movement, anything unnatural, any disruptive pattern that does not fit in with the surroundings, and anything that shines will cause a second look to be taken.

Fit your position into the natural background and do not try to make natural surroundings fit your position.

www.ingramcontent.com/pod-product-compliance
Lightning Source LLC
Chambersburg PA
CBHW060225050426
42446CB00013B/3172